From the acclaimed author and founder of UPI...

SHEPHERD COACH

UNLOCKING THE DESTINY OF **YOU** AND YOUR **PLAYERS**

Shepherd Coach: Unlocking the Destiny of You and Your Players

COPYRIGHT © 2018 TOM ROY

All rights reserved. No part of this book may be used or reproduced by any means, graphic, electronic, mechanical, including photocopying, recording, taping, or by any information storage retrieval system without the written permission of the author except in the case of brief quotations embodied in critical articles and reviews.

Scripture quotations marked (NLT) are taken from the Holy Bible, New Living Translation, copyright ©1996, 2004, 2015 by Tyndale House Foundation. Used by permission of Tyndale House Publishers, Inc., Carol Stream, Illinois 60188. All rights reserved.

Scripture quotations taken from the New American Standard Bible® (NASB), Copyright © 1960, 1962, 1963, 1968, 1971, 1972, 1973,1975, 1977, 1995 by The Lockman Foundation Used by permission. www.Lockman.org

Scripture quotations are from the ESV® Bible (The Holy Bible, English Standard Version®), copyright © 2001 by Crossway, a publishing ministry of Good News Publishers. Used by permission. All rights reserved."

ISBN: 9781729574188

FOR VOLUME DISCOUNTS OF THIS BOOK FOR YOU OR YOUR ORGANIZATION CONTACT:

PULPIT TO PAGE PUBLISHING CO.
ORDERS@PULPITTOPAGE.COM

PULPITTOPAGE.COM

From the acclaimed author and founder of UPI...

SHEPHERD COACH

UNLOCKING THE DESTINY OF **YOU** AND YOUR **PLAYERS**

"I respect Tom's ministry as much as I respect **any** ministry around the world. My endorsement for him is at the top of the list."

— Chris Singleton, ESPN Analyst and former MLB Player

TOM ROY

TO CONNECT WITH TOM ROY
VISIT ONLINE OR **WRITE TO**:

1247 FREEDOM PARKWAY

WINONA LAKE, INDIANA 46590

TOMROY.NET

CONTENTS

INTRODUCTION 1
1 | WHAT IS A COACH? 3
2 | MOTIVATION 5
3 | MY JOURNEY 9
4 | PHILOSOPHY 13
5 | THE BATTLE 15
6 | MENTOR 17
7 | DISCIPLE 21
8 | SHEPHERD 27
9 | COMMITMENT 33
10 | LEADERSHIP 37
11 | TRUTH 43
12 | GETTING STARTED 47
13 | CHALLENGES 53
14 | DYSFUNCTION 61
15 | RELATIONSHIPS 65
16 | T-R-M 73
17 | MAKING DISCIPLES 79
18 | THE WALL 87
19 | TOOLS 105
20 | CHARTS 113

INTRODUCTION

Hey, Coach! How's it going? I don't know what series of events in your life led you to become a coach, but that's what people call you. You may be coaching a high school or college team, a youth league or church league team, or possibly an individual sport. You want to make a difference and be a positive influence with your athlete or athletes. But you are finding there is more to coaching than athletic training.

The purpose of this book is to guide you into understanding that your role as a coach is a God-given position. It just might be the most important opportunity in your life, the chance to have a life-changing impact on young men and women.

I have had the privilege of coaching at several levels, from youth to college athletes, in both Christian and secular schools. During those years, I observed the style of many great coaches like Vince Lombardi, Bobby Knight, Tom Landry, John Wooden, Pat Summitt, Tony Dungy, and many others. Coaching styles and philosophies vary, but all are aimed at motivating young athletes toward their peak performance.

If you are a man or woman who considers yourself a follower of Jesus Christ, coaching is a noble calling. Have you ever wondered if the principles

Jesus taught apply to your coaching? Which coaching philosophies are valuable? Which coaching styles should be avoided?

My prayer is that your eyes will be opened to the unique position God has given you. Jesus called himself the Good Shepherd. As a coach, you are also a shepherd. You have a flock and you are responsible for guiding the sheep that have been entrusted to you.

HOW TO READ THIS BOOK

Before you begin, please fill out the charts at the back of the book. This will give you a point of reference as you work through some of the details discussed.

CHAPTER ONE
WHAT IS A COACH?

Hello, fellow leaders of men and women! No matter what level or sport you are coaching, you are leading future leaders. They come with a variety of backgrounds, attitudes, personalities, and abilities. Your responsibility as their coach is to hone their individual athletic skills and mold them into the best athletes they can be. Your goal is to teach them not to settle for good, but to strive for best.

At every level, there is pressure to win. Hopefully, coaches of young athletes are able to focus more on teaching the fundamentals of the sport. However, parents and fans who want their athlete to succeed can put pressure on coaches to win, even insulting and threatening the coaches.

At the university level, job security often depends on the number of wins. Pressure can come from the conference, the athletic director, or the institution itself. At the professional level, there is pressure from owners and financial backers to produce a winning team because winning equals profit. There is the added pressure of the media, which analyzes and scrutinizes every decision of the coach.

Coaching is a high calling and it comes with much pressure and high demands. But is there more to coaching than training athletes to achieve athletic success? What does it mean to be a shepherd coach? Can the leadership style of Jesus be applied to coaching? Will it help or hinder athletes to succeed? Is it even possible in an environment where others have no interest in anything but winning?

Let's dive into this issue! Although this book will not answer every question about coaching, it will guide our thinking into more than just the X's and O's of the sport.

CHAPTER TWO
MOTIVATION ...why do you coach?

Have you ever asked yourself this question? There are many possible reasons. Here is a list to get you started:

- I was a good athlete and coaching made sense
- I love working with kids
- I love seeing a team come together and watching it develop
- It is the only thing I know how to do
- I feel pressured to coach
- I need the extra money
- Coaching feeds my ego
- My child is an athlete and coaching provides a chance to do something together
- I see coaching as my passion and calling in life
- I miss playing and this is the closest I can get to that
- I happened to fall into the job
- My spouse likes that I coach
- It provides an income for my family
- I love the relationship with other coaches

- I love to teach
- I love to be in control
- I love the title
- It's an honorable profession

This list is not complete, but is designed to get you thinking about your motivation for coaching. Most coaches have more than one reason for coaching and many have a number of reasons. There are no right or wrong answers here; only *your* answers. Feel free to fill in the blanks below with some of the reasons for the drive behind your coaching:

_____
_____
_____
_____

WHY DO YOU COACH WHERE YOU DO?

What was the reason for choosing the level or location of your coaching? For some of you, this might be an easy question. For others, you may have never considered it. Maybe you fell into the job and never gave it any thought. Here are a few possible answers:

- The pay is good
- I like the school/program

- I like the leadership/administration
- I like the location
- We have a winning program
- We have good players coming up the ranks
- I am just a dad and this level fits my skill set
- I like the uniform colors
- I like the schedule
- My kids are here
- It's a good fit for my family
- This is a stepping stone to the next level
- This is a destination coaching position
- I have no reason to leave
- I like the atmosphere
- I love the energy of the fans
- This is a good group of kids
- I am building a legacy
- I am building a culture

Again, this is not a complete list, but take some time to think about it. For another perspective, talk with your spouse if it helps. Why you have chosen to coach where you are may be as important as why you coach. It can add a piece to the puzzle. Take a minute to write down your thoughts. It will help you remember!

YOUR TURN!

CHAPTER THREE
MY JOURNEY

Before we continue, allow me to share a little of my journey with you. At the age of seventeen, I signed with the San Francisco Giants organization, injuring my throwing arm and getting released. That experience did much to shape my coaching philosophy.

My first official coaching position was as an 8th grade basketball coach. It was a blast working with these young kids. The next year I started a youth football team in our town. We went undefeated and I caught the coaching bug.

I then went on to a coaching position as a pitching coach at a small Midwestern college. I loved it! I showed up, worked on the fundamentals of pitching with the staff, and loved game day. My philosophy at that time was to be a good assistant and advocate for the head coach, be a dedicated learner and instructor of pitching, and instill confidence in the pitchers.

Prior to signing, I had very little instruction on preventing injury, and I became dedicated to learning all I could about pitching and passing that on to the pitchers. I believed in being focused, running a tough practice, and correcting flaws while building confidence. I desired to see the pitchers believe in their ability and experience success. Game day was cheering the young men from the dugout while evaluating what changes needed to be made.

After three years at that position, I was approached by a local high school about applying for the head baseball job, as well as coaching junior varsity basketball. As it turned out, I was hired and also became the offensive coordinator for the football team! That job interview caused me to begin seriously developing my philosophy as a head coach.

I was a young believer in Jesus applying for a job at a public high school. I believed I needed to come up with a philosophy that lined up with the teaching of the Bible without violating public school policy. My goal was to apply principles that honored God, expressed in a way that would make sense in the public sector.

I loved coaching and knew in my heart it was what I was built to do. But I also did not want seventeen-year-old kids determining if I had a job! I prayerfully attempted to develop a philosophy of coaching that would allow me to be judged not only on my performance but also on how I taught and how I related to and believed in the kids. High school coaches are not typically in a position to recruit talent, so you work with the talent that comes up through the system. You play the hand you are dealt.

After quite a bit of soul searching, I came up with a philosophy that I felt would accomplish my goals. Here it is:

- People are more important that program
- Program is more important than winning
- Winning is important

My first priority was people. I wanted to be evaluated on how I handled the athletes above everything else. I couldn't openly discuss my faith with the team, but I could care for the kids. I wanted to build a family environment and a community of care.

My second priority was building a program for the athletes. I would need to stay ahead of the kids in my research and understanding of coaching. I would need to run organized, disciplined practices and teach the fundamentals of the game. I would need to select assistant coaches carefully and teach them how to be better at their jobs. I needed to be a coach, not simply putting together a lineup.

My final priority was winning. I most definitely wanted to win! Whenever a scoreboard was involved, I put forth my best effort, within the rules, to win. I expected the same from my players.

Write out your coaching journey. By documenting your path, it may help you understand how God has led in your life.

_____

_____

_____

CHAPTER FOUR
PHILOSOPHY

If you took a college coaching class, chances are you were given an assignment to write out your philosophy of coaching. But like other things in life, we get busy and lose focus on why and how we want to lead as a coach.

It's your turn. What is your coaching philosophy? Give it some thought and prepare to write it down. It's important to have a philosophy for coaching, but while you're at it, keep in mind that it's a good idea to be able to articulate a philosophy for life – for your marriage, family, career, and personal goals.

At the end of the book, there is a questionnaire to help you develop a personal mission statement. It will help you stay true to who you are and why you coach. Try to make your coaching philosophy as short and easy to remember as possible. Mine is 20 words, but I can get it down to 3: PEOPLE, PROGRAM, WINNING.

YOUR TURN!

_____
_____
_____
_____
_____

CHAPTER FIVE
THE BATTLE

News Flash: We are all in the same battle. We live in a performance-based culture where worth is determined by titles, numbers, and dollars. As coaches, we can fall into that trap, believing our worth is measured by the scoreboard or the statistics.

Ever since the battle recorded in the third chapter of Genesis, people have battled with pride and the need to perform. It is important to understand this battle and recognize that true worth is not defined by performance. It is defined by who we are as believers in Christ.

As coaches, our job is to train our athletes to perform at the peak of their ability. We tend to define our personal success by how well they perform. That's normal and natural for a coach.

But God has called us to the supernatural. How are we supposed to reconcile the difference? Is it possible to redefine our priorities without compromising excellence in coaching? What if you could integrate your faith into your philosophy of coaching? What if you could influence your athletes toward excellence in life as well as athletics? Remember, our assignment is different than our identity.

I believe it is not only possible, but it will take your program to an entirely new level. You, Coach, have the potential to have eternal influence in the lives of young men and women!

We need to redefine what a win looks like!

In your own words, write out what a win should look like for you and your team.

YOUR TURN!

_____
_____
_____
_____
_____

CHAPTER SIX
MENTOR

Now that you have developed a baseline for why you coach, let's move on.

A number of years ago I heard an analogy that has stuck with me to this day:

What is the difference between the game of Checkers and the game of Chess?

Answer: The goal of Checkers is, jump you, king me. The goal of Chess is to think several moves ahead to protect the king.

This analogy makes sense to me in the contrast between the world system and God's system. The world system is Checkers, but God's way is more like Chess. Rather than thinking about personal gain, God calls us to think about others.

Another interesting point about the analogy is that both games are played on the same board! Too often, we divide our lives into separate segments as if we are playing life in different arenas. We cannot separate our Christian lives from our jobs! Our faith needs to play out in every arena!

As followers of Jesus, our manual for life is the Word of God. It is the truth that guides our lives. But how does that translate to coaching? There is no specific teaching about coaching athletics in the Bible. However, there are many powerful lessons on leadership that can be integrated into our job as coach. These principles have the potential to transform an ordinary coach into a shepherd coach.

Like it or not, coaches are mentors for young men and women in sports. Author Bob Biehl explains the importance of this in his book Mentoring: "Mentoring is the emotional glue and is the relational glue that can hold our generation to the last and to the next. Mentoring is the relational bridge connecting, strengthening and stabilizing future generations of Christians."

A mentor is a trusted counselor or teacher. Coaches have the opportunity to mentor athletes simply because of their position. I understand many of you are not in situations where you are able to openly speak about your faith. You can, however, demonstrate your faith in the way you coach!

There is a misconception that being a follower of Jesus is not desirable for athletes, as it will make them less committed and competitive. You have an opportunity to model that the opposite is true. In fact, as believers in Christ, we are compelled to always give our best effort!

Please hear my heart. I understand some of this may seem simple, but I am constantly amazed at how few coaches actually apply these concepts. There is no shame here! Many of us were not coached by men who understood how to mentor athletes in both life and sport. Most of us simply don't know how.

YOUR TURN!

Who are you currently attempting to mentor?
_____
_____

Who comes to mind as someone to start the process?
_____
_____
_____

Who were your mentors?
_____
_____
_____

*Perhaps it's time to write them a note of thanks?

CHAPTER SEVEN
DISCIPLE

Let's zoom in on the idea of a disciple. How does a shepherd coach make disciples? What does that mean? What is a disciple?

The New Testament frequently uses the word disciple, referring to the followers of Jesus. When a coach models excellence in life as well as in athletics, he is a mentor. When a coach models how to be a follower of Christ, he is making disciples, and that is what a shepherd coach does!

The Greeks used the term to refer to a learner, or on a more committed level, an adherent. As an authority in the lives of your players, your responsibility is to teach, inspire, and motivate them to work hard, learn all they can, and love their sport so they can play at the best of their ability.

As a shepherd coach, the level is elevated. The title 'Coach' gives you a unique opportunity to model what it looks like as an athlete to have a relationship with Jesus. As you pursue your own relationship with him, you will be representing Jesus to your players. They will see him in you and in the way you coach, and he will become more real and tangible to them.

Just as there were disciples in the Greco-Roman world of the first century, there were disciples in Judaism, as well, who were committed to a recognized leader or movement.

"There is evidence that personal discipleship was carried on among the Greeks and the Jews. Though the term 'disciple' is used in different ways in the literature of the period, there are examples of discipleship referring to people committed to following a great leader, emulating his life and passing on his teachings. In these cases, discipleship meant much more than just the transfer of information. Again, it referred to imitating the teacher's life, inculcating his values, and reproducing his teachings" (www.bible.org).

Jesus called certain men to follow him and he specifically chose twelve disciples to be his disciples. He wanted them to know him and enjoy him. A shepherd coach does much the same thing: he shows athletes how they can know Jesus and enjoy him.

First Corinthians 11:1 says, "Be imitators of me, just as I also am of Christ." As followers of Jesus, this is a high calling, to imitate Jesus, especially in the competitive world of sport. But as leaders of young men and women, this is our calling.

Mark 10:42-45 says, "Jesus called them and said to them, 'You know that those who are recognized as rulers of the Gentiles lord it over them, and those in high positions use their authority over them. But it is not this way among you. Instead whoever wants to be great among you must be your servant, and whoever wants to be first among you must be the slave of all.

For even the Son of Man did not come to be served but to serve, and to give his life as a ransom for many.'"

As a coach, you demand exclusive, complete, and unflinching obedience to your program. Jesus, your coach, demands the same from you. This means you are his servant in the world of sport. Yes, Coach, you are there to serve your players. The idea of serving may be a foreign concept to some who are accustomed to 'lording it over' their athletes. However, a shepherd coach can follow Jesus' model of teaching, coaching, serving, and loving each athlete without compromising one bit of the competitive spirit.

The call to discipleship is not without its challenges. As a coach, you are already giving up a lot of your time. The idea of taking it a step further and serving your athletes probably sounds like too much. But it's not about us, Coach. It's about the athletes. That is what shepherd coaching looks like.

Our job is to lead athletes to their limit, mentally and physically. Our goal is to put forth the best possible performance with the athletes entrusted to us. Our calling is to pour into their lives, giving them spiritual tools to equip them for life. Yes, it's a big challenge. But Jesus gives us this encouragement: "Don't be afraid, for I am with you. Don't be discouraged, for I am your God. I will strengthen you and help you. I will hold you up with my victorious right hand" (Isaiah 41:10, NLT).

He will provide the strength and direction you will need. As you spend time with Jesus, listening to him as you read his Word and talking with him in prayer, he will guide you in how to disciple your players.

This is what Jesus wants us to do! In Matthew 28:19, he says, "Therefore, go and make disciples of all nations." It is part of the call of every believer in Christ to make disciples. Jesus asks us to live our lives in a way that the players are attracted to him. When they begin to follow us as we follow Jesus, we are making disciples. If you aren't sure about all this talk of mentoring and discipleship, may I challenge you to consider the words of Jesus calling us to make disciples? If it's important to him, it's important.

In summary, a disciple of Jesus is someone who has been called to know Christ, to follow him, to make disciples of others. Making disciples is the calling and privilege of a coach. Coaches often talk about developing a culture within their sport. What if that culture was a culture of discipleship? What if you, as a coach, decided to proactively model the teachings of Christ in your environment?

YOUR TURN!

In your own words, write down your understanding of what it means to be a disciple and to make disciples. In later chapters, we will discuss ideas on how to accomplish this.

_____
_____
_____
_____
_____
_____

SHEPHERD COACH

CHAPTER EIGHT
SHEPHERD

I once heard a story about a Middle Eastern man who was explaining to a friend the role of a shepherd. The true shepherd leads his sheep. He continued telling of how the shepherd goes ahead, prepares the way, and cares for the sheep. Just then, the student looked up to see a number of sheep pass by. The problem he saw was that the shepherd was not in front, but rather in the back of the pack. The young man raised his hand and asked the teacher a question. "You mentioned that the good shepherd leads his sheep. I just saw a group of sheep with the shepherd in the back of the flock." The teacher looked in the direction of the sheep and responded. "Young man, that is not the shepherd, that is the butcher."

To understand what it means to be a shepherd coach, we need to understand what it means to be a shepherd. Jesus called himself the Good Shepherd. Here is what he said, in his own words:

"Very truly I tell you Pharisees, anyone who does not enter the sheep pen by the gate, but climbs in by some other way, is a thief and a robber. The one who enters by the gate is the shepherd of the sheep. The gatekeeper opens the gate for him, and the sheep listen to his voice. He calls his own sheep by name and leads them out. When he has brought out all his own, he goes on ahead of them, and his sheep follow him because they know his voice. But they will never follow a stranger; in fact, they will run away from him because they do not recognize a stranger's voice."

Jesus used this figure of speech, but the Pharisees did not understand what he was telling them.

> Therefore Jesus said again, "Very truly I tell you, I am the gate for the sheep. All who have come before me are thieves and robbers, but the sheep have not listened to them. I am the gate; whoever enters through me will be saved. They will come in and go out, and find pasture. The thief comes only to steal and kill and destroy; I have come that they may have life, and have it to the full.
>
> "I am the good shepherd. The good shepherd lays down his life for the sheep. The hired hand is not the shepherd and does not own the sheep. So when he sees the wolf coming, he abandons the sheep and runs away. Then the wolf attacks the flock and scatters it. The man runs away because he is a hired hand and cares nothing for the sheep." (John 10:1-13)

In this conversation, Jesus mentions four types of people: the shepherd, the stranger, the thief, and the hired hand. How does this apply to coaching and which person describes your style as a coach? Here is my take on what each of these four types represent:

The Shepherd is the coach who teaches truth and who deeply cares for his athletes as people. He oversees by leading and his purpose is not to be a king, but to make kings.

The Thief is the coach who uses his position for personal gain. He or she is only interested in himself or herself.

The Hired Hand works for the pay and will do no more than is required. The hired hand is motivated to win because it means a pay raise. The attitude is, "They don't pay me enough to get involved with these kids."

The Stranger does not care about anything but the sport. These coaches will teach the X's and O's of the sport, but that's it. They expect the athletes to grow up on their own.

Which type best describes your style of coaching? How would your athletes describe you? Do they see you as a hired hand or a stranger? Do they see you as a thief or a shepherd? If your players were interviewed, which of the following statements would they use to describe you?

- If I need to talk, Coach is there for me.
- I did not know my coach was a Christian.
- My coach's faith does not translate onto the field.
- Coach motivates me to be better in life as well as in my sport.
- Coach is only in it for himself.
- Coach is knowledgeable about my sport.

- Coach has clear expectations.
- Coach pushes me out of respect.
- Coach sets a good example.
- Coach is relational.
- Coach invests in players on and off the field.
- Coach pushes me hard, but I know how much he (or she) cares about me.
- Coach is demanding.
- I'm afraid of making a mistake because Coach will humiliate me.
- Coach is like a father (or mother) to me.
- Coach only cares about winning.

Well, Coach, how did you do? Is it time to rethink your approach to coaching?

Coaching is not an easy job. You may be thinking of the hours invested in preparation, teaching, correcting, and practicing in addition to coaching. Developing a culture of caring may seem like more time and work than you are willing to invest. You may feel there are not enough hours in a day to truly become a shepherd coach.

If you suspect your athletes view you as a thief, a stranger, or a hired hand, what are you willing to do to change the culture where you coach? You are in a position to shepherd your athletes to become world changers!

Question: Would you say your team sees you as a shepherd or a butcher?

If the concept of becoming a shepherd coach sounds overwhelming, let me encourage you that changing the culture of coaching is not about longer practices or tougher schedules. It's not about changing your to-do list. It's about a change in motivation. It begins by thinking of yourself as a shepherd coach and realizing the unique privilege entrusted to you. You have been given the opportunity to influence young athletes at a pivotal time in their lives. It's an adjustment in thinking.

"Don't copy the behavior and customs of this world, but let God transform you into a new person by changing the way you think. Then you will learn to know God's will for you, which is good and pleasing and perfect." (Romans 12:2, NLT)

God is the one who transforms how a shepherd coach thinks. A shepherd coach doesn't follow the leadership style of most coaches, but follows the leadership style of the Good Shepherd.

Adjustments may need to be made to your coaching style if you desire to be a shepherd coach. Change will come as God's truth gets inside you and transforms your thinking. The Word of God is the coach's playbook where the Head Coach gives instruction for you as his shepherd coach.

Still with me, Coach? Hang in there! I believe what's ahead will be helpful to you and your program.

List when you have acted like a:

Thief:
_____
_____
_____

Hired Hand:
_____
_____
_____

A Stranger:
_____
_____
_____

A Shepherd:
_____
_____
_____

What changes do you need to make as a result of the above analysis?

CHAPTER NINE
COMMITMENT

I am convinced if you embrace the concept of becoming a shepherd coach, it will have a tremendous impact on your program as well as your individual players. However, Coach, it has to begin with you being a disciple of Jesus. The following is a prayer written by Dan Britton, published in FCA magazine.

THE COACHES PRAYER

Lord, when I pick up the whistle, lace up my shoes and walk out of the locker room, I coach for You alone. There is no turning back. In every victory and every defeat, I celebrate Your goodness and greatness. The way I coach demonstrates my love for You. I stand for the cross and declare my loyalty to You. I coach for You.

My energy and enthusiasm come from the Holy Spirit. My purpose and passion come from above. Through the strain and struggle, I never give up or give in. The champion inside of me is Jesus who gives me strength. Winning is honoring You in all I do. I coach for You.

When I coach, I feel Your pleasure. My heart longs for Your applause alone. All of my abilities are from You. I am under Your authority as my Ultimate Coach. I will respect and honor all competitors, coaches, and officials. I compete by all of the rules. I coach for You.

My coaching is my offering to my Savior. I am Your warrior in the heat of battle. I am humble in victory and gracious in defeat. I coach to serve You, my athletes, and our opponents. My words bring healing and refreshment that inspire and motivate. I speak words of life. I coach for You.

Success isn't a winning program, but seeing the power of Christ transform the lives of my athletes. Victory is not the scoreboard, but for my athletes to become more like You. Bless my athletes in great ways and increase their faith and confidence. I coach for You.

In the name of Jesus, I pray. Amen.

Remember, lift up your athletes through prayer daily. God will use your prayers to transform lives. Pray well. Coach well.

This prayer articulates the heart of a shepherd coach. Did any part of it stand out to you? Did it call your attention to any area of struggle for you as a coach? Did it encourage you to coach with a shepherd's heart? If it was helpful, I encourage you to make a copy and keep it where you will see it often.

Use the following space to write out your reaction to this prayer. In what ways do you struggle as a coach? What part of this prayer inspired you? What action do you intend to take? What changes do you plan to make in your program?

If you prefer, use the space to write out your own prayer:

_____
_____
_____
_____
_____
_____
_____

Over the years, I've had the privilege of speaking with a number of coaches and teams about the idea of becoming a shepherd coach. The following are some of the ideas these players and coaches have recorded:

- Service projects
- Guest speakers
- Organize leader-conducted Bible studies
- Lead weekly Bible studies

- Practice pre-game prayer
- Go to church together
- Care for players to open doors to share
- Offer game day chapels
- Pray before practices
- Schedule one-on-one meetings
- Ask for prayer requests from players
- Post scripture verses in the locker room
- Make Christian books available to players

If you are coaching in a secular environment, you will not have as much freedom to speak about your faith, but you may find a few ideas that will work for your program. Be creative, Coach!

CHAPTER TEN
LEADERSHIP

Speaking of being creative, here are some specific ways you can build up your athletes as a shepherd coach. According to research done by The Flippen Group, we all have the following five basic human needs:

1. Security
2. Community
3. Clarity
4. Authority
5. Dignity

As a coach, you have the potential to help build up your athletes in each of these areas of need. A shepherd coach is intentional about this, and the result is that strong relationships are built and athletes tend to stay in touch long after their playing days. When that is the case, a true shepherd coach will give the credit to Jesus in a way that is understood and received.

If you are coaching a professional team, it becomes a little more challenging, especially in the area of security. Your athletes are professionals who are expected to produce results. It's a business that involves players getting called up, sent down, or traded, and you don't have final control of their job security. The goal of the player is to climb the ladder and there are always younger, faster, and better players waiting to take their job. However, you have the opportunity to build up your players in the other four areas.

Here is my take on how these five needs can be addressed by most coaches:

SECURITY: Create a team mentality, where everyone on the team is important, not just the players who are regular starters. Each player practices with the team. Each player contributes something and adds value to the team. All of us are better than one of us.*

COMMUNITY: Create a sense of community on the team, where players care about each other. Encourage team social events and community service. Create situations or events where team members have to work together and challenge each other. Encourage healthy competition, but discourage anything that is negative or divisive. Model what it means to speak the truth in love, both on and off the court or the playing field.

CLARITY: It is the responsibility of a coach to clearly articulate what is expected from players in practice, in game situations, and off the field. If communication is not your strength, ask your assistants for help. Being clearly understood is essential.

SHEPHERD COACH

AUTHORITY: As the coach, the buck stops with you. Your players need to know that. Authority is a double-sided responsibility. Coaching is an honor, but it also means making the tough calls at times. You need to let your players know you believe in them and in the team, but you are the one to make the difficult decisions based on what is best for the team, even if they don't understand.

DIGNITY: A coach needs to always keep in mind the dignity of every individual. Part of the job of coach is to teach and correct, adjust and challenge. As a coach who is a follower of Jesus, the goal is to do that in a way that never demeans or diminishes the dignity of the athlete. Coaches can help athletes believe in their potential and motivate them to work harder and hone their skills without damaging their dignity. The individual is more important than the goal.

YOUR TURN!

You are a leader and your thoughts are valuable, so give this some thought. How do you see ways to build up your athletes according to these five needs? What do you plan to implement into your program? Be specific. Write your thoughts on the following page:

_____

_____

_____

_____

_____

_____

_____

One of the challenges for coaches is finding the balance between authority and caring. Being a shepherd coach does not mean you become a player's best friend. There are several thoughts on this topic, but what are your thoughts? How do you maintain your position of authority while shepherding your players?

This is an important topic and I urge you to have this discussion with your assistants, if you have them, and with other coaches and leaders. For sure, good communication plays a role, but there is value in gathering ideas from others. Every athlete is unique. Every coach is different. We can learn from each other.

No coach wants to be average! If that were the case, they wouldn't bother to put in the effort it takes to be competitive. A shepherd coach is a leader with passion and a strong work ethic who expects nothing less than an athlete's best effort. A shepherd coach leads by example and believes actions will influence others and drive outcome. It's up to you, Coach, to find your own way to lead with strength, without compromising your authority, while finding ways to care for and shepherd your players.

A final thought to consider in this discussion on leadership is your relationship with the families of your players. You may have players from homes where one or both parents are absent or dysfunctional. Very frequently, a coach is looked up to as a parent figure by a young athlete or his family. One way you can care for your athletes is by reaching out to their families and fans. In fact, this might be one of the best possible ways to care for your athletes. Who knows what opportunities might come up! Maybe you could include them by keeping them updated on the team schedule, events, and records through an email or Facebook group. What are some other ideas for ways to include the families and fans of your athletes?

CHAPTER ELEVEN
TRUTH

WHAT IS TRUTH?

Pilate asked this question of Jesus, and today, many people are asking the same question. We live in a society that questions authority and rejects absolute truth. Many define truth as whatever they believe is true for them and consider the concept of universal truth as narrow-minded and discriminatory. This may present one of the biggest challenges for you as a shepherd coach and may present a roadblock to making disciples.

Fortunately, in athletics, there is a greater understanding of absolute truth in terms of discipline, schedules, and rules of the game. Authority is represented by coaches and referees or umpires.

WHAT DO YOU BELIEVE?

Your first challenge is to know what you believe. Many who identify as believers in Christ have a life philosophy that is a mixture of biblical truth and current cultural beliefs. What do you believe? Do you believe there is absolute truth?

Secondly, do you believe God's Word is truth? Proverbs 30:5 says, "Every word of God is flawless; he is a shield to those who take refuge in him." Do you believe every word of God is flawless?

Third, do you believe Jesus is the truth? He claimed to be. "Jesus answered, 'I am the way and the truth and the life. No one comes to the Father except through me'" (John 14:6). That's a bold statement.

If you believe Jesus is the ultimate truth and every word of God is flawless, then the Bible is your authority in every area of life, including coaching. As you apply the truths of the Bible to your coaching, you can have confidence it is true and good.

"Do your best to present yourself to God as one approved, a worker who does not need to be ashamed and who correctly handles the word of truth." (2 Timothy 2:15)

WHAT IF I MESS UP?

The Word of God is flawless, but coaches are not! In the heat of the game, it isn't unusual to say or do things that are later regretted. One of the most powerful tools of a shepherd coach is the power of apology. A true leader is willing to admit being wrong and offer a sincere apology. It shows players their coach is human and it speaks louder than any speech. It takes humility and authenticity from a coach. It is a powerful teaching tool and trust builder.

HOW DO I LEAD LIKE JESUS?

"Instead, speaking the truth in love, we will grow to become in every respect the mature body of him who is the head, that is, Christ." (Ephesians 4:15)

You can probably remember coaches or teachers who had a lasting impact on your life. Coaches have a rare opportunity to invest in young lives. I can't stress that point enough! You have hard-earned gems of wisdom that your players may never learn anywhere else. You are in a position to express the truths of Jesus as you interact with them on a day-to-day basis. You may not be able to freely talk about it, but you can live it!

One way to do that is to speak the truth in love. This means honesty and authenticity, not compromising or sugarcoating the truth. However, it also means speaking in a way that your athletes know you truly care about them and you want what is best for them.

Truth is powerful, and young people are incredibly discerning about truth.

Jot down any thoughts that come to mind after reading this chapter:

_____
_____
_____
_____
_____
_____
_____

CHAPTER TWELVE
GETTING STARTED

LEADING LEADERS

Many of you coach alone, which means you carry all the responsibility for your players. Most likely, you have a team captain or captains. If you coach a team sport, you may be a head coach or an assistant coach. As a head coach, you divide the responsibility among your assistants according to the specific position they coach. As an assistant, your responsibility is to train a particular group of players to maximize their skills so they can contribute to the team and help win games. Either way, you are a leader of leaders.

THE JESUS MODEL

Just as you choose players for your team, Jesus chose twelve men to be his disciples. He focused on them; teaching them, preparing them, and praying for them. In coaching terms, he laid out his philosophy to these leaders to pass on to others. He could have taken a different approach by simply meeting the needs of the crowds. After all, everyone needed his life-changing touch. But Jesus was training his disciples to reach the world! He understood the importance of leaving a legacy that would continue for generations. His winning strategy was simple. For three years, he trained his disciples to "go and make disciples of all the nations" (Matthew 28:19).

Those of us who call him Lord are also called to go and make disciples. As a coach, you are already in a position of training leaders. You have a specific amount of time to invest in their lives. How are you going to use your position to coach like Jesus coached? Let's take a look at the Jesus model.

- Jesus carved out time for intimacy with his Father. (Mark 1:35; Luke 4:42)
- Jesus prayed specifically for his disciples. (John 17:6-19)
- Jesus recruited his disciples and gave them his vision for leadership. (Matthew 4:18-22; Luke 5:1-10)
- Jesus invested personally in his disciples—heart-to-heart. (John 6)
- Jesus related to non-believers. (Mark 2:13-17)
- Jesus gave his disciples opportunities to minister to others like he did. (Luke 9:1-6)

"He who believes in Me, the works that I do he will do also; and greater works than these he will do, because I go to My Father." (John 14:12)

This is a pretty big promise and it is for you! Possess it as your own. When you build on the foundation of Christ's authority rather than your own, you will be able to coach at new levels!

We are all called to make disciples. Who does God want you to disciple? Is it your assistant coaches? Is it your team captains? Maybe it is time for a coaches' meeting to discuss your direction and philosophy. You may want to meet with each of your assistants individually to offer them discipleship in order to be able to disciple others. Let's take another look at the quote by Bob Biehl in his book Mentoring:

> "Mentoring is the emotional glue and is the relational glue that can hold our generation to the last and to the next. Mentoring is the relational bridge connecting, strengthening and stabilizing future generations of Christians."

I like the term mentoring when referring to cross-faith connections. As followers of Christ, our goal is to make disciples who will mentor others to make disciples.

LEAVING A LEGACY

Is it your desire to leave a legacy of disciples who follow Christ as you follow Christ? What would you say is your legacy at this point in your coaching career? How would your team answer that question? How about other coaches or fans? Would they describe you as a good coach with a great work ethic? Would they talk about how you love Jesus and teach his ways? Hopefully they would say both are true!

YOUR TURN!

Look over the following questions and write your answers in the space below. Answer the best you can and include any other thoughts you have, like potential problems or obstacles to becoming a shepherd coach. Do you have questions or concerns? What do you fear? What might be the advantages to your coaching program? Be as honest as you can. This will be good for you now as well as an evaluation tool to return to at the end of each season.

1. How do you conduct coaches' meetings?
   _____
   _____
   _____

2. What are your priorities with your assistant coaches?
   _____
   _____
   _____

3. How do you relate to other coaches?
   _____
   _____
   _____

4. What changes would you like to make?
   _____
   _____
   _____

5. What holds you back from implementing change?

_____
_____
_____

6. Are you ready to share your vision for a culture of discipleship?

_____
_____
_____

7. If you decide to follow Jesus' model of coaching, what is at stake for you?

_____
_____
_____

CHAPTER THIRTEEN
CHALLENGES

Coaching comes with built-in challenges. You have elevated levels of competition in your life and elevated expectations on you. Some coaches coach for the love of the game and some for the love of athletes. Hopefully you know your reasons and hopefully both are true! Whatever your reasons, there are challenges that come with the job.

The main challenges I've identified are worth, record, pride, and relationships. Whether you are a follower of Jesus or not, we all face the same battle, as we discussed in chapter 5. The good news for believers in Christ is the presence of the Holy Spirit for help in facing these challenges.

WORTH

Maintaining a sense of worth is a challenge for men who derive their sense of worth from their position, performance, or income. In recent years, it seems women are also struggling more with the same issue. Our identity is tied to our career. We have allowed our current culture to define our worth based on what we do rather than who we are.

Jesus has a different definition of worth:

By this we know love, that he laid down his life for us, and we ought to lay down our lives for our brothers. (1 John 3:16)

Basically, by laying down his life for us, Jesus is saying we are worth it! Our value to him is that we are worth dying for. This is the opposite of our cultural view of worth! And he doesn't wait for us to be good enough.

But God demonstrates his own love for us in this: While we were still sinners, Christ died for us.
(Romans 5:8)

The only way to win the battle of worth is to base it firmly on what God says. His Word does not change. Otherwise, personal worth is subject to every win, pay raise, promotion, and pressure to prove our worth. Because we are human, we need to constantly remind ourselves of this truth. However, this in no way allows for giving anything less than one hundred percent where competition is concerned. But we need to remember that only Jesus determines our worth.

This is a difficult concept for coaches to grasp. Coaching is driven by performance and an expectation to win. The following verse may be helpful:

"God has not given us a spirit of fear and timidity, but of power, love and self-discipline." (2 Timothy 1:7)

That's a great combination-- power and discipline with love! That's a great description of a shepherd coach!

If you forget everything else you read in this book, Coach, please remember to never let anything or anyone but Jesus determine your worth. He thinks you're worth everything!

The theme for my life has been: It's great to be alive because God is in control. Enjoy coaching, be the best coach you can be, and let God determine the results.

RECORD

Another area of struggle is losing. Coaches hate to lose. No coach wants a losing record, so the bar is set high. The goal might be conference champions, regional pride, state or national rankings, or world titles. Coaches need to set the bar high to give athletes a goal to focus on and a desire to make the sacrifices necessary to win. A winning record is the goal!

This area of challenge could fall under the topic of worth, but I believe it deserves some attention by itself. If a winning record is the goal and the goal is not met, how does a coach respond in the face of failure? What if every effort has been made to produce a winning record but it simply did not happen? What if a coach's job is at risk? How does a shepherd coach move forward when fired?

It is helpful to have a philosophy of coaching, especially when coaching high school students or younger. If the philosophy has been laid out and followed, a losing record may not be the only criteria for evaluation, but the job may still be at risk. At the collegiate and professional level, we've all seen good coaches and godly men fired after losing seasons. It's much easier to fire a coach than rebuild an entire team. To return to the question, how does a shepherd coach move on when fired?

The answer goes back to worth. A shepherd coach is not defined by a winning season. A shepherd coach gives the best effort possible and trusts God with the results. If he defines worth and if he is in control, we have to believe he has allowed a losing season and a job loss for a reason. He is sovereign and we need to trust he knows what he is doing. It may be his way to move us forward to better things. The following verses help put this in perspective:

"Many are the plans in the mind of a man, but it is the purpose of the Lord that will stand." (Proverbs 19:21, ESV)

"'For I know the plans I have for you,' says the Lord. 'They are plans for good and not for disaster, to give you a future and a hope.'" (Jeremiah 29:11, NLT)

"And we know that in all things God works for the good of those who love him, who have been called according to his purpose." (Romans 8:28, NIV)

A coach is called to give the best effort possible. Our personal effort is the only thing we control. Many years ago, I heard a concept called ACE and I've used it many times when speaking to athletes. ACE is an acrostic that represents the three things we can control:

ATTITUDE

"Have the same attitude as Christ" (Philippians 2:5).

CONCENTRATION

"Forgetting the past and looking forward to what lies ahead" (Philippians 3:13).

EFFORT

"Whatever you do, work at it with all your heart, as working for the Lord" (Colossians 3:23).

This concept can be applied when a coach is in a situation of being evaluated. There are only certain areas that we can control. You can control your attitude. If you have given your best effort, you can feel good about that. And you can forget the past and look forward to what is ahead. Yes, coach, you may be fired for reasons beyond your control, but there are still things you can control.

By the way, this concept works well in other areas of life, such as marriage. Who wouldn't want to be married to a coach who applies these things to life?

PRIDE

Much of what we have discussed has its base in pride, and we all naturally live at that address at times.

Jesus calls us to change our address to super-natural. He gives the ability to see life from his perspective and to live for a greater cause than ourselves. Pride is our default setting and we will continue to wrestle with pride as long as we live. I am not minimizing the challenge of that battle. Often our flesh screams louder than the Spirit in us. Pride is strong in all of us, but God gives us his Spirit to overcome the tendency to give in to pride.

"For the flesh desires what is contrary to the Spirit, and the Spirit what is contrary to the flesh. They are in conflict with each other, so that you are not to do whatever you want." (Galatians 5:17)

RELATIONSHIPS

Another area of struggle is often in relationships. Family, fans, or the media can be very challenging! Consider the response after an athletic event, especially if it didn't go well. Words can be hurtful. Fans can be extremely vocal and harsh, especially during the heat of the game. Family can be angry and critical, especially if their family member didn't get the playing time the family thinks they deserve. And the media can tear a team apart and throw the coach right in there with them.

Responding with defensiveness or with anger never helps. In fact, it can escalate the situation. A heated situation gives a shepherd coach an opportunity to set an example and rise above the negativity. That's easy to say, but much harder to do in a heated situation. It's essential for a coach to take a minute to mentally prepare before responding. Say a short prayer asking Jesus to help regain perspective before answering critics or giving interviews. Those moments are when we will build the fabric of true identity.

It's great when a coach has a family that is supportive, but that isn't always the case. After facing negative reactions in public, a coach needs to come home to a positive environment. If that is not the situation, it might be time for an honest conversation. Behind hurtful words are hurting people. It's possible the demands of coaching have pulled focus away and the needs of family members have been forgotten. In a healthy family, each member is important. Sometimes simply listening to each other promotes understanding and empathy.

Responding poorly at times is inevitable. When a coach is humble enough to admit it and take responsibility for it, it can have an even greater impact than a good response. There have been many times I've 'lost it' and had to apologize to my team as well as officials, fans, and media. My actions and my words did not represent who I am and what I believe. As difficult as it was, I had to ask for forgiveness.

An example of this happened early in my coaching days. Failure is part of life, but sometimes failure presents a unique opportunity. I had taken a college team to play the University of Hawaii at Hilo. I believed we were getting 'homered' and totally lost it with the officials. After venting, I began to feel terrible and the Holy Spirit kept nudging me to apologize. Finally, I asked the opposing coach if I could speak with his team. He agreed and I could see his players tense when I walked into the locker room. They didn't know what to expect, but looked stunned when I asked their forgiveness for my outburst. Later, several of them privately expressed the impact that had on them. It was a lesson I've never forgotten.

These four challenges are common, but may not be the only areas of struggle. Use the space below to write out your biggest challenges. How do you approach these challenges? What ideas have you gained for facing your challenges? You may want to discuss this with other coaches who are followers of Jesus and share your ideas on how to win these battles.

_____
_____
_____
_____

CHAPTER FOURTEEN
DYSFUNCTION

Most families have some type of dysfunction. Why would it be any different within the framework of a team? Given the home situations of many athletes, it's understandable when athletes have difficulty with attitude, focus, or relationships. The Five Dysfunctions of a Team by Patrick Lencioni gives some interesting insight into how dysfunction affects a team. The five areas of dysfunction he has identified are:

1. Absence of trust
2. Fear of conflict
3. Lack of commitment
4. Avoidance of accountability
5. Inattention to results

Absence of trust often translates as an attitude of invulnerability. For a team to gel and work together, vulnerability and trust are imperative. Team members must be open and honest with each other and be committed to having each other's back. Trust is the foundation of the team, and without it, the framework of the team will crumble in the heat of competition. It may stay below the surface as long as the team is experiencing success, but as soon as the team begins to lose, the disunity will become evident. The challenge for the coach is to create a healthy environment of trust, where athletes feel free to discuss strengths and weaknesses honestly and openly.

Fear of conflict causes artificial harmony. Peace is not the absence of conflict but the resolution of truth in a godly manner. This is great advice for newlyweds, but it applies to teams as well. As a coach, you probably already realize conflict is not necessarily bad. Sometimes conflict is avoided at the expense of truth. A wise coach allows athletes to discuss and disagree respectfully and learn how to handle conflict with maturity. This is "speaking the truth in love" (Ephesians 4:15). Athletes who stay silent because of a fear of conflict will kill their chance for resolving conflict and developing deep friendships.

Lack of commitment means ambiguity. If athletes are not allowed to weigh in, most likely they won't buy in. Players may salute your title but not believe in you or your program. They may appear to agree, but if they are afraid to voice their thoughts or if they don't feel heard, they may not be on board.

Avoidance of accountability will lower the standards of the team. Honesty and openness means being willing to be held accountable. Accountability is a must for both the team and the coaching staff. When there is no accountability, there is no opportunity to learn from our mistakes. As a coach, be sure there is a process of accountability in place.

Inattention to results is about ego and status. Where there is a lack of trust, healthy conflict, commitment, or accountability, winning or losing doesn't matter to the athletes. Individual performance and statistics are what matter to them. They are playing for themselves, not the team. They don't care about the results as long as they looked good.

Here are some questions to get you started. Use the space below to answer. Remember Coach, this is not a quiz! These questions are designed to be tools to help you evaluate your personal coaching staff and player interaction. They are designed to help you become a shepherd coach.

As a coach, how would you evaluate your coaching staff or your team, based on these standards?

_____
_____
_____

Most coaches have a program and goals. Are your athletes invested?

_____
_____
_____

How well do you listen to the ideas and concerns of your athletes? Do they believe in your program and do they believe they can contribute to the team?

_____
_____
_____

Are your athletes able to resolve conflict in a healthy way? Is there unity on the team?

_____
_____
_____

Do you have a process in place for accountability?

_____
_____
_____

What is the level of commitment on the coaching staff? How about the athletes?

_____
_____
_____

CHAPTER FIFTEEN
RELATIONSHIPS

If you have coached for any amount of time, you realize the need for a healthy distance in the relationship between you and your athletes in order to maintain respect and authority. This is especially true for young coaches who are not much older than their players.

If you are a Junior High or a High School coach, especially if you live and coach in a small community, relationships can present challenges. Parents may accuse the coach of giving their favorite athletes more playing time or special privileges. Athletes suspect other athletes are given favor if their parents are friends with the coach or if they come from a wealthy or prominent family in the community. It can also be a sticky situation if you are known as a follower of Jesus and some of your athletes are not. You may be viewed as playing favorites based on faith, either by players or parents.

Hopefully these are not factors in making decisions as a coach. Relationships cannot be allowed to cloud rational judgment. If this is a problem and you have found yourself giving in to pressure, adjustments need to be made to be sure all players are given equal consideration.

A shepherd coach needs to find the balance in developing healthy relationships without compromising authority and equality. It may be helpful to meet with other Christian coaches and listen to how they handle similar tensions. Whatever the situation, a coach is called to care for athletes as Jesus would.

In the Word of God, we find how to have a relationship with our Creator. It also sets the standard for relationships with others. How does that play out as a coach? Allow me to offer a few suggestions for cultivating healthy relationships within coaching.

LET THEM KNOW YOU CARE

At the beginning of the season, find a way to communicate to your athletes, and their parents if appropriate, your goals and your philosophy of coaching. Let them know you care for them off the field as well as on the field. Let them know you will be available if they need to talk. This could be accomplished with a team meeting or possibly an email.

SET HEALTHY BOUNDARIES

Communicate when you will be available so your time is not abused. You may want to set specific office hours or times for phone calls. Your family may not appreciate a call at 2am! Depending on your situation, you may feel it is best to communicate only with your athletes and let them communicate with their parents. My purpose is not to tell you what to do, but to encourage you to set parameters early.

MEET WITH ATHLETES

During the season, I encourage coaches to set up meetings with each athlete to get to know them better. If you have a large team, or if this is not your strong suit, your assistant coaches can share the responsibility. I especially encourage meeting with team captains. This will help get a sense of the temperature of the team and gain insight into personalities and attitudes. It also provides an opportunity to invest in them and let them know what you expect of them as team leaders.

USE TECHNOLOGY

Technology can be an extremely helpful tool in nurturing relationships. I suggest creating a group email to keep all athletes informed and updated on schedules, practices, and team events. A Facebook page can be a great way to send photos and keep family and friends in the loop on game highlights, scores, team events, fundraisers, etc. Technology can also be used to assist spiritual growth by sending verses, quotes, and devotional material. Again, this can be delegated to an assistant coach.

A shepherd coach has a responsibility to be relational with each athlete. They are young and they need a shepherd. In any discipleship model, we are called to "feed the hungry and love those who are not." This is especially true in coaching.

Below are some questions to keep in mind as you meet with your players. They can be useful in understanding and evaluating each individual athlete to know where they may need guidance in their sport and in life.

- How do they handle free time?
- How do they handle stress?
- How do they respond to adversity?
- How do they manage their time?
- Do they have a need to be in control?
- What are their interests?
- Do they get adequate rest?
- How do they respond to criticism?
- How do they respond to authority?
- How do they handle money?
- Can they direct their competitive nature?
- Do they value integrity?
- How do they respond to being given gifts? (Do they have an entitlement attitude?)
- Are they a team player?
- Do they accept responsibility when they are wrong?
- How do they handle fear?
- How do they handle loneliness?
- Are they patient?
- Are they loyal?

- What are their weaknesses?
- What are their strengths?
- Are they sensitive to others?
- What motivates them?
- Are they moody?
- Are they insecure?
- What life situations have shaped them?
- What are their personal goals?

Remember, we were built for relationships. How you listen is as important as how you lead. Get to know your athletes on a human level and you will find out much about why they respond the way they do. Who knows, your athletes might teach you something! My good friend Jerry Price says, "None of us are as smart as all of us."

As a shepherd coach, you lead by example. The book of Galatians includes a great list of attributes of a shepherd coach:

"But the fruit of the Spirit is love, joy, peace, patience, kindness, goodness, faithfulness, gentleness and self-control." (Galatians 5:22-23)

All of these attributes are a result of the Spirit of God working in us. Self-control might just be the toughest one, especially in tense game situations! But a shepherd coach sets the standard for athletes to follow. This might be a great time to evaluate which 'fruit' needs tending!

YOUR TURN!

Young athletes need strong leaders who care about them and who are able to shepherd them in life. In my first book, Released, there was a section on leadership which I have included below. As you look this over, ask yourself what God might be showing you. I would love to hear from you! Please feel free to email me your thoughts and questions at troy@upi.org

- Be positive: Caleb saw the potential when others did not
- To compare is an error
- God is in control
- Heart, vision, and passion are vital for godly leaders
- Choose character over ability and experience
- FLO = Be FAITHFUL, LOYAL, OBEDIENT
- Ministry is both being ministers and administers
- Is my yes a yes – James 5:12
- Be strong and courageous
- Be Bold - Psalm 16:8
- Have a critical eye rather than a critical spirit
- Our thinking determines our emotions which determine actions
- Love equals obedience
- Dependency is built on trust
- When wronged, our best defense attorney is Jesus
- Accept responsibility

- You may be hated without reason - John 15:25
- I am small but HE is big
- When you have a setback, sit back before you comeback
- STAR - Straight Thinkers Accept Responsibility
- We are all just broken lambs
- Develop persistence and resistance - persistence to persevere and resistance to mediocrity
- Develop discipline and dedication
- There is a difference between power and influence
- Slow cooking means more tender…Time is your friend, not an enemy
- Stay HOT - Humble, Obedient, and Teachable
- Leadership style: David, Saul, or Absalom?
- Wash feet…an attitude of a servant
- We can choose to be bitter or better
- Practice quick repentance - Isaiah 14:12
- There is a fine line between confidence and arrogance
- Learn to delegate
- Allow people to fail at times as failure is a great teacher
- Emotions are good, but they are spice, not meat
- Learn to listen to older saints - they have battle scars
- Be an example, leave a positive legacy
- Work within your gifts

What practical steps can you begin to establish in your program?

_____

_____

_____

_____

_____

_____

CHAPTER SIXTEEN
T – R – M

How does a shepherd coach relate to a player who does not have a relationship with Jesus? The T-R-M principle is a helpful tool in this situation. T, R, and M stand for Truth, Relationship, and Mission.

TRUTH

As followers of Christ, truth needs to be the standard in every conversation, whether it is with players, fans, parents, or the media. Today's athletes have been marinated in a culture that teaches truth is relative. Absolute truth is rejected and personal truth is promoted. The truth is adjusted according to the situation. However, authentic relationships are built on truth.

Culture has changed, but truth has not. For the believer in Christ, truth is found in the Word of God. Jesus said, "I AM the truth" (John 14:6), meaning every word he speaks is truth. When opportunities come to speak about personal faith, the Word of God is our source of truth.

The Word of God is also powerful and able to cut through to the heart. Hebrews 4:12 says, "For the word of God is alive and active. Sharper than any double-edged sword, it penetrates even to dividing soul and spirit, joints and marrow; it judges the thoughts and attitudes of the heart."

When we speak the truth from Scripture, it wields more clout than our own words.

This doesn't mean there can be no fun on the team! Storytelling and humor are healthy. Most coaches enjoy sharing war stories. However, there is a time for serious discussion and speaking into the lives of the athletes with biblical truth. It is the responsibility of the coach to set aside time for these conversations.

The coach sets the tone for the team. For coaches who want to make a difference and possibly introduce athletes to Jesus, it's important to make it a priority to get familiar with God's Word. Then, if an opportunity comes to speak with an athlete about Jesus, you are ready. The Spirit of God will bring to mind a verse you have read recently that applies to the conversation and you will be able to speak truth with confidence.

Coaching is a position of influence. It's easy to get into conversations about sports, politics, etc. My challenge is to look for opportunities to speak about the truth of Jesus, especially with those who do not have a personal faith.

RELATIONSHIP

The title of coach carries with it a position of authority. A shepherd coach is called to build relationships with players without compromising authority. As believers, we have the privilege of asking the Holy Spirit for wisdom in how to use that position. Many athletes lack healthy authority figures in their lives. They have learned to be guarded and mistrustful of authority. A shepherd coach can set an example of an authority figure who lives authentically, who cares about them, and who deserves their respect.

Coaching provides many up close opportunities to get to know athletes personally and learn about their struggles and their dreams. There is a time for teaching, correcting, and disciplining, but there will also be appropriate times to listen and to speak encouragement. Athletes need to know their coach believes in them. There will also be opportunities to speak about faith. It's important to be alert and ready for those open moments.

Every coach has a different style and there is no such thing as one style fits all. God will open up opportunities to speak about salvation. A shepherd coach has earned the right to speak into the lives of their athletes based on the relationship that has been established. When there is an open door with athletes who do not have a personal faith or belief in God, the conversation will be a natural extension of the relationship. A shepherd coach can simply be who they are and speak from their own experiences.

It is possible to have athletes who show no interest in spiritual conversations and do not show appreciation or respect. It has been my experience that over time, those athletes come to respect a coach that speaks truth into their lives and who also lives it. Relationships built on the truth of the Word of God are very important. God's truth is powerful, even many years later.

MISSION

Every coach has a mission in coaching. A coach is responsible to train athletes to become excellent in their sport. A shepherd coach has a mission also. Shepherd coaching will include teaching life values and encouraging excellence in character. A shepherd coach will likely need to define different missions with individual athletes. The entire mission for one athlete might be showing the love of Christ. For another, it might be leading them to Jesus, while others may need to understand how to mature in their faith.

In public speaking, it's important to define the mission and to stay on mission. My mission as a speaker is to always give Jesus the glory. Sometimes that is not the mission of the group that has asked me to speak! In those situations, I need to honor those who invited me and trust that something I say or the way I say it will cause people to ask me about what I believe. The same is true in coaching. There will be situations where it is not allowed or appropriate to speak about personal faith in Jesus. In these cases, we can ask God for wisdom on what to say and he has promised to answer that prayer! "If any of you lacks wisdom, you should ask God, who gives generously to all without finding fault, and it will be given to you" (James 1:5).

Coaching is an opportunity to be an influencer. It is up to you, Coach, to ask God how you can have an eternal influence in the lives of each of your athletes. Use the space below to write your thoughts.

How can I communicate God's truth into the lives of my athletes, verbally or nonverbally?

_____
_____
_____

How can I develop relationships with my athletes? How can I teach them healthy respect?

_____
_____
_____

What is my mission with my team?

_____
_____
_____

Write the name of each athlete on a separate line. Write a personal mission statement for each one.

_____
_____
_____
_____
_____
_____
_____
_____

CHAPTER SEVENTEEN
MAKING DISCIPLES

For most of this book, we have been setting the table. Now it's time to talk about the X's and O's of discipleship. We serve a very creative God and we will follow his model. I'm guessing many of you have ideas to add and I would love to hear how you go about God's business of discipleship with your team! You will find my contact information in the back of the book.

THE 1-3-12-5000 MODEL

This model is not my idea and it is not new. It was modeled by Jesus and has been followed by many. It is based on the relationships of Jesus. Jesus had thousands of followers, but he chose twelve to specifically become his disciples. Out of those twelve, three were close and one was especially close. He invested in those twelve, teaching them daily as they lived life together.

As a shepherd coach, what if you viewed your team this way?

Following this model, you would choose one athlete to invest in at the deepest level. This would probably be an upperclassman and very likely the team captain. You would be intentional about spending time with this individual, teaching biblical truth. This could be accomplished by meeting weekly or more often if necessary. Timothy tells us to pass on to faithful men what we have learned. Your job would be to identify who you believe will be faithful.

The next group would be the three who would make up your inner circle. They would be athletes you desire to invest in and would likely also be upperclassmen and team leaders. They could include your number one choice or be three other athletes. You would meet with them as a group once a month to discuss how to integrate faith and life, using the Bible as a study guide.

Twelve represents the team as a whole. This could involve team meetings, weekly Bible studies, praying together, praying on the field, or sharing testimonies within the team while together.

The five thousand represents the public. This could include families of players, fans, and people in your community. It might also include audiences if you speak publically or have opportunities for interviews on radio or television. These are opportunities to speak about your faith in Christ to the public.

THE A-B-C-D MODEL

This is another model of discipleship. With this format, I try to evaluate where each player on the team is spiritually. I realize this can be subjective, but once you have some idea about the spiritual health of each individual, you can adjust where each one fits.

The A's would be those who are on fire for Jesus. They have a solid biblical foundation, they are sold out for Jesus, and they can't get enough of his Word.

The B's are individuals with a personal faith in Jesus but don't yet understand how powerfully faith can affect daily life.

The C's are infants in their faith. They have made a commitment to Christ at some point in their lives, but it has never become part of their lives.

The D's do not have a personal faith in Jesus. Some do not understand and others don't want anything to do with Jesus.

This may not describe everyone, but it gives a starting point. You are already teaching your coaching staff, and when you add assistant coaches to the mix, you could have quite a diverse group! As the leader, you will need to decide your strategy with each group. This may help to see them as individuals and not one big group.

This tool can help you be more intentional in what and how you teach. You may want to enlist the help of your assistant coaches in creative thinking and planning. Depending on your situation, you might want to give some of your A athletes some leadership responsibilities in discipleship. The question is how to be Jesus to your athletes. The goal is making disciples.

BRICKS OR KITES

I came up with the terms "Bricks" and "Kites" on a mission trip. There were a number of guys on the trip with various backgrounds and levels of commitment to Jesus. The "Kites" were the guys that wanted to fly with Jesus. He was the wind and they wanted to soar with him.

The "Bricks" were the ones who were satisfied with staying on the ground spiritually. They didn't want to be moved and they weren't useful for much. Let's face it, most teams have both kites and bricks! We need to discern how to best reach them and use them.

THE DIVIDE AND CONQUER MODEL

This model divides your team into groups. With input from your staff, you decide the criteria. You could divide by class, position, or whatever fits your team. You know your team and the backgrounds of both players and coaches. Use that knowledge to put these groups together. A fun way to do this is have a draft party. The purpose of this is to pick your discipleship team. The picks will be under your leadership for the year. You will plan times to get together as a group, meet individually, and personally pray for each of them. You may even decide to invite them to your home. It's up to you, Coach! Whatever it takes to make disciples!

U-C-L-A

No, this is not a university in California. This acrostic stands for UpperClassman Lead Approach. I saw this at a college where I once coached. Here is how it works.

At the beginning of each year, you gather your top Junior and Senior athletes. In a different setting, you decide which athletes are your leaders. My point of reference is college, so please understand my position in expressing how it worked.

Once you have identified your leaders, ask them to look over the list of underclassmen, including new recruits. They will then decide how to divide that group equally, giving each of them leadership responsibilities for the entire year. If these leaders are followers of Jesus, they can be stretched to disciple their group of underclassmen with prayer, Bible study, etc.

If they are not followers of Jesus, they can still lead by looking after their group and sharing life with them. This can include showing them around the campus, helping them with homework, and sharing resources with them. During this time, they will give you feedback on those in their group, letting you know how they are doing. You can learn more about their personalities, strengths, and weaknesses. You will be able to make suggestions to your leaders on ways to encourage their group. At the same time, you will be developing deeper relationships with your leaders. This model will help you develop the team culture you desire and it gives your leaders ownership by giving them leadership responsibilities.

THE 'I CARE' MODEL

This model is great because it singles out individuals for one-on-one time. It includes motivated A's, or Kites, who invest in one other person's life for a year. They meet face-to-face for meals, homework, Bible study, or life talks, all for the purpose of discipleship.

Allow me to illustrate with an example. A player on a college team made a commitment to another player who was not a follower of Christ. He opened his apartment to him on a weekly basis. He found out this individual really liked spaghetti and meatballs, so he invited him for dinner. Other nights, he prepared other favorites. Now that is true commitment! The intent was to have deeper relationship. He was up front about the fact that the purpose for getting together was to talk about life issues from a biblical perspective. After more than a year of inviting this teammate over and openly talking about his faith, that teammate trusted in Christ as his Savior. The 'I Care' model obviously takes an athlete that is committed to the process of being Jesus to his teammates.

These are just a few models for discipleship. I'm sure there are more. If you've found other methods, I would love to hear from you! The purpose is to stretch your players spiritually.

PRAYER

Whatever your model, there is nothing more powerful than prayer. Some coaches lead in prayer before or after games. Some include prayer in team

Bible studies. If your athletes know you are praying for them, it will be meaningful to them. If they hear you praying for them, it will have a lasting impact on them. "The prayer of a righteous man is powerful and effective" (James 5:16).

Which of the models above best suits your situation? How could you implement it into your program? Use the space below to describe what you think would be a good plan of discipleship for your team.

_____
_____
_____
_____
_____
_____

Ask each of your athletes how you can pray for them. List their names and prayer requests below and remember to pray for them. Ask for updates.

_____
_____
_____
_____
_____
_____

CHAPTER EIGHTEEN
THE WALL

The first time I had the opportunity to speak about shepherd coaching, I found an interesting article about the stages of spiritual growth: "Spiritual Formation: The Hagberg-Guelich Model of Stages in the Life of Faith." The authors defined the stages of the journey based on a survey they conducted. I have included a summary of six stages in this chapter. I believe it is helpful for us as coaches to identify the stage of our own spiritual journey and set goals and prepare for the next stages.

STAGES OF THE JOURNEY

Stage One: Recognition of God

Stage Two: A Life of Discipleship

Stage Three: The Productive Life

Stage Four: The Wall

Stage Five: The Journey Inward

Stage Six: The Journey Outward

At some point in our lives, we are faced with a decision. We come to a turning point and we choose to follow God or go our own way. We come to faith in God or we trust in ourselves. We begin a journey to know God or we live our lives as if we are our own god. In either scenario, we come to recognize the need to understand the eternal.

So here is a question: When did you personally decide to follow Jesus and what were the circumstances that led to this choice? Have you ever written out your story? Have you ever verbalized your testimony to your team or in another public setting?

Once we start this journey with God, we should notice several changes taking place in our lives. When we come to the point of realizing there has to be something more to life than simply existing, we start to understand that what we are missing is God. We begin to understand how God sees us. At one time, I believed God's love for me was based on what I did for him. I thought when I messed up, he was angry with me, and when I performed well, he was happy with me. According to God's own words, that simply isn't true.

"Therefore, there is now no condemnation for those who are in Christ Jesus, because through Christ Jesus the law of the Spirit who gives life has set you free from the law of sin and death." (Romans 8:1-2)

What does no condemnation mean? It means once you are in Christ, you are loved unconditionally!

STAGE ONE: RECOGNITION OF GOD

Stage one is when we realize our need for a Savior. We can never be good enough to earn salvation. There is a sense of awe at the realization that all is forgiven. When we turn from our old ways and turn toward him, Jesus removes sin and shame. What follows is a great sense of freedom and purpose. He lifts burdens and frees us to live openly and honestly.

"For the wages of sin is death, but the gift of God is eternal life in Christ Jesus our Lord." (Romans 3:23)

"It is for freedom that Christ has set us free. Stand firm, then, and do not let yourselves be burdened again by a yoke of slavery." (Galatians 5:1)

"'For I know the plans I have for you,' declares the Lord, 'plans to prosper you and not to harm you, plans to give you hope and a future.'" (Jeremiah 29:11)

"Forgiveness is the greatest miracle that Jesus ever performs. It meets the greatest need; it costs the greatest price; and it brings the greatest blessing and the most lasting results." (Wiersbe)

Before giving our lives to Jesus, most of us based our self-worth on how we acted on our best days. We ignored our worst moments and had a higher opinion of ourselves than our actions merited. But underneath there was a fear that we were not good enough. This thinking creates an identity crisis.

HURDLE

A transformation of our thinking must take place or we will get stuck questioning our worth and believing God is angry with us. As Romans 12:2 says, our minds need to be transformed. The cross is God's statement that we are worth dying for. He loves us that much and our worth is based on that love.

Another important factor is community. Coaches, if we are to develop as followers of Jesus, community is crucial. We are not meant to be on a spiritual journey alone. It's possible to attend church and still be isolated. It's important to get plugged in and surround ourselves with other believers. Let's consider ourselves part of Team Jesus!

We each need a "Paul," a "Barnabas," and a "Timothy" in our lives for us to be successful in our journey with Jesus. Paul was a teacher and mentor. Do you have a mentor or someone who is teaching you the ways of Jesus? Barnabas was an encourager. Do you have an encourager in your life? Do you have friends who tell you the truth and not just what you want to hear? Timothy was a student, a young believer. Your players are each "Timothys" in your life. You will be better able to teach and mentor them if you have teachers and encouragers in your own life.

STAGE TWO: A LIFE OF DISCIPLESHIP

Coach, have you ever been discipled? We discussed this in a previous chapter. Discipleship is when a mature believer teaches a new believer what it means to follow Christ.

"Anyone who belongs to Christ has become a new person. The old life is gone; a new life has begun!" (2 Corinthians 5:17, NLT)

When we become followers of Jesus, we know we belong to him, but we don't know how to live this new life. We need someone to walk beside us and teach us the ways of Jesus.

"Those who say they live in God should live their lives as Christ did." (1 John 2:6)

Making disciples is not just a suggestion or a good idea for followers of Jesus, it is a command.

"Jesus came and told his disciples, 'I have been given all authority in heaven and on earth. Therefore, go and make disciples of all the nations, baptizing them in the name of the Father and the Son and the Holy Spirit. Teach these new disciples to obey all the commands I have given you. And be sure of this: I am with you always, even to the end of the age.'" (Matthew 28:18-20, NLT)

Jesus doesn't just offer salvation and move on. He promises to always be with us. We live in a culture where we have unlimited information and we want everything instantly. But spiritual growth takes time. We need Jesus to mature us and we need someone to walk beside us to show us the ways of Jesus. This doesn't happen instantly. But as we are discipled, we become equipped to disciple others.

Jesus set a perfect example for discipleship. He taught his disciples as they lived life together. As we are discipled, we will be equipped to disciple others. As you interact with athletes on and off the field, you will be modeling a life of faith. You may not be able to speak openly about your faith, but they will see your attitudes and your actions. They will see that verse you keep on your desk or the way you care about them each personally.

HURDLE

One of the potential pitfalls to our growth is comparison. Discipleship is an individual journey. No one can do our growing for us. As followers of Christ, we need to keep our eyes on him and not on others.

When we compare, we can become rigid and judgmental of others or self-righteous, thinking we are better than others. As disciples of Jesus, we listen for what he asks of us and we leave others in his capable hands.

When we disciple our athletes, we don't compare them with each other. We get to know each personality. It has been said that rules without relationship will equal rebellion. Just as we train our athletes to reach their maximum potential based on their individual abilities, we encourage them in their spiritual journey based on their individual personalities and needs.

We must celebrate how God has uniquely wired each of us. We must find our worth in Jesus and believe what he says about us. We must learn his ways and teach them to others. God will use each of us if we honestly and humbly seek him.

"You have heard me teach things that have been confirmed by many reliable witnesses. Now teach these truths to other trustworthy people who will be able to pass them on to others." (2 Timothy 2:2, NLT)

This is discipleship.

STAGE THREE: THE PRODUCTIVE LIFE

"But don't just listen to God's word. You must do what it says. Otherwise, you are only fooling yourselves." (James 1:22)

This stage of the journey is about living what we believe. We are followers of Christ and we are being discipled. Now we need to act on what we have learned. This stage is both exciting and challenging.

You know you belong to Jesus. You have learned the importance of staying connected to other believers. When you don't have fellowship with others, you are hungry for it. You are not satisfied to just sit in church; you have a thirst for more. Your journey with Jesus is spilling into other areas of your life and that is a sign you are maturing in your faith.

This did not happen all at once. You have seen the value of spending time with Jesus, reading the Word, praying, and spending time with other believers. People have begun to notice a difference in the way you respond to tough situations. You have begun to understand the importance of investing in things that last. What you value will determine how you will spend your time.

"Wherever your treasure is, there your heart and thoughts will also be." (Matthew 6:21, NLT)

HURDLE

We live in a performance-based world. The world's philosophy tells us to put ourselves first and we can get stuck in that mentality. When performance is central, hope is placed on what performance can deliver. The problem is that even when we reach maximum performance, we find it doesn't totally satisfy us. It's never enough. No amount of wins can satisfy like living life with Jesus!

Getting stuck at this stage can be rough. We are moving from trying to please God to trusting God. If we catch ourselves thinking we have arrived at a level of spiritual maturity, we need to remember it is Jesus who is working in us. He gets the credit! This understanding allows us to serve rather than be served. This is the way of a shepherd coach.

"People may be pure in their own eyes, but the Lord examines their motives." (Proverbs 16:2)

STAGE FOUR: THE WALL

The Wall is a place of crisis. Most of us hit the Wall at some point in our spiritual journey. It may be triggered by loss or tragedy and it shakes us to the core of our beliefs. It may be caused by our own sin, shame, or pride. It may be a result of exhaustion or self-effort or people-pleasing. Whatever the cause, life is not working the way we thought it should and we run head first into the Wall. All our church attendance and good works seem meaningless and we question our faith. We stop pursuing our relationship with Jesus.

Blaise Pascal wrote, "God made man in his own image and man returned the compliment." It takes a profound conversion to accept that God is relentlessly tender and compassionate toward us just as we are--not in spite of our sins and faults, but with them. Though God does not condone or sanction evil, he does not withhold his love because there is evil in us.

Whatever the reason for our personal Wall, our human nature makes us prone to hide from God rather than running toward him. This is exactly where the enemy wants us – stuck in a place of hopelessness. We move into anger, depression, or self-hatred. We believe lies and reject truth.

"The thief's purpose is to steal and kill and destroy. My purpose is to give them a rich and satisfying life." (John 10:10)

When we hit the Wall, we must hold on to what we know to be true of God and let go of everything else. I believe one reason we hit the Wall is we try to move too quickly through Stage Two. We try to "do" for God rather than learn what it means to "be" with God.

HURDLE

Getting through the Wall is not easy. It requires surrender, forgiveness, risk, repentance, honesty, vulnerability, love, and movement toward God. If we have been walking with Jesus for a while and have worked hard to build an image, bringing our struggles and doubts into the light sounds terrifying. But what's the alternative? Staying stuck? Continuing to live behind a mask and keeping others at a distance? If that's our choice, we will never get through the Wall. Honesty is essential. Vulnerability is frightening, but necessary. The freedom and joy on the other side are worth it!

We need help getting through the Wall. Our spiritual journey was never meant to be solo.

"Confess your sins to each other and pray for each other so that you may be healed. The earnest prayer of a righteous person has great power and produces wonderful results." (James 5:16)

It's good and healthy to find someone we trust to confess to when we have hit a Wall. If we have put up walls and kept people out, it may be difficult to find someone to confide in. However, it is essential to seek someone we believe is trustworthy. Who knows, maybe that individual is looking for someone like you; someone safe to confide in!

Don't get stuck on words like "sin" and "repent." Sin simply means missing the mark and we all miss the mark many times a day. Repent means to turn; turn away from sin and turn toward Jesus.

"Come close to God, and God will come close to you." (James 4:8)

Sometimes the Wall is not a place of crisis but of complacency. We have grown comfortable and comfort requires no risk. It focuses on satisfying selfish desires. We have worked hard to arrive at a place of comfort with safe, predictable lives and great vacation packages. We have become addicted to comfort and we have no desire to push through the Wall into the unknown. This is another form of faith crisis.

Our journey with Jesus is the greatest adventure and the most unpredictable ride possible! It is a continual test of faith and it may or may not be "safe." As tough as it may be to push through the Wall, it will be more than worth it.

It's very possible we will hit more than one Wall. If we push through, there may be another Wall in the future. If we stay connected to Christ and stay humble, he will get us through and grow us in the process.

STAGE FIVE: THE JOURNEY INWARD

If we have pushed through the Wall, whatever that looks like, we have been stretched in our faith and have experienced God at a deeper level. But we realize there is more. Stage Five is about starting the process of moving toward authenticity. It requires taking an honest look inward. We all fear exposure, so we act like everything is fine, even when it is not. We have a fear of being known for who we truly are. Our human nature wants to project an image of success and confidence, especially with the title of Coach.

"Whoever walks in integrity walks securely, but whoever takes crooked paths will be found out." (Proverbs 10:9)

As a coach, we are paid to have answers. But living authentic lives means we don't have to have all the answers! For true change to take place, we must pursue authenticity and integrity. Jesus does not ask us to perform miracles. In fact, it's not about performance. He asks us to trust him and engage with him. He will mature us. Who knows, he might just perform a miracle through us!

We are never going to be perfect, and our athletes will never be perfect. We don't have to wear a mask of perfection. As coaches, although we are in a position of authority, we must understand that we can humbly trust Jesus with our imperfections. We can discuss any issue with him. He promises he will never stop working on us. It is his job to complete us and perfect us.

"And I am sure of this, that he who began a good work in you will bring it to completion at the day of Jesus Christ." (Philippians 1:6, ESV)

HURDLE

Discipline is part of coaching. We want to set an example of discipline for our athletes and we expect discipline from them. But discipline may be where we as coaches get stuck in our spiritual lives. When discipline becomes the central focus in our spiritual lives, it becomes all about following rules and self-effort. Discipline in itself is not wrong, but if we get stuck living by rules, we will miss the intimacy that comes with spiritual freedom.

Because athletics is performance based, there is a great possibility that we are attempting to earn God's approval through our performance. This mindset will smack us head first into the Wall. Understanding our motives is what will help us over the Wall. We already are approved because of Jesus. There is nothing more to earn. We are free to enjoy our relationship with Jesus.

We can also get stuck in self-centeredness, which is a brutal beast. A key to getting unstuck is recognizing this trait dwells deep within all of us. Getting unstuck will take understanding, asking for forgiveness, and possibly extending forgiveness.

STAGE SIX: THE JOURNEY OUTWARD

The acrostic TEA stands for Thoughts, Emotions, and Actions. Our thoughts affect our emotions, our emotions affect our actions, and our actions determine the direction of our lives. It all begins with our thoughts. What we believe determines how we live our lives.

For most of us, coaching is our identity. I'd like to suggest coaching is our assignment, not our identity. Our identity is found in Jesus. The journey outward is understanding who we are in the eyes of Jesus and living from that understanding.

Before each of us was born, God knew everything about us. Jeremiah 1:5 says, "Before I formed you in the womb I knew you, before you were born I set you apart." Jesus placed so much value on us he thought it was worth his death to have a relationship with us. It has nothing to do with what we have accomplished. We are his treasure! If we understand nothing but this one thought, it will change our destiny. We move from trying to perform well enough to earn God's approval to learning to trust who he says we are.

It is at this stage we develop a true heart for others and desire deep and authentic relationships. We begin to grasp the concept of being truly surrendered to God's purpose for our lives. We believe him and we trust him. We become more focused on what is best for others rather than ourselves. This is when we begin to become shepherd coaches!

HURDLE

Hopefully by now we don't get stuck nearly as often. However, it's still possible to be misunderstood. When we exhibit peace in a stressful situation, it can be misread as not caring. When we don't panic or blow up, we can be seen as lacking passion. As we grow in our faith, the normal storms in life don't blow us off course as easily because we trust in God's plan. Losses still hurt and negative press is painful. But our identity is no longer based on our win/loss record or criticism in the media. We know who we are and we know we are treasured.

When we have a solid relationship with Jesus, we have the privilege of relaxing, knowing he is completely in control even when life seems out of control. We need to be prepared. Some people will be encouraged by observing our faith, but others will be skeptical. We may face some opposition.
As we grow in our faith and learn what it means to live it, we will grow in our hunger for God's Word.

The Word is God speaking to us. It is how we get to know him. The more we get to know our God, the more we long to know him better. The more we realize he has our best interest at heart, the more we want to involve him in every detail of our lives.

The more we get to know God, the more prayer becomes a vital part of our lives. It is a conversation with our God. It is both speaking and listening. It is a privilege we have because of Jesus. Sin in our lives put a barrier between us and God, but the cross broke the sin barrier. Just as communication is vital in marriage, so is regular communication in our relationship with God. The more we discern the voice of God in our lives, the more we desire to listen and hear from him.

YOUR TURN!

After reading the six stages of the life of faith, where would you place yourself?

_____
_____
_____

Do you have a fear of being truly known? How can you overcome a fear of exposure?

_____
_____
_____

What is your motivation for living the Christian life? Is it success or acceptance? Is it a desire to look good to others?

_____
_____
_____

Why is forgiveness so difficult? Are there people you need to forgive?

_____
_____
_____

List the name of anyone you need to forgive. Include your own name if you have trouble forgiving yourself. Use a separate sheet of paper. Ask God to help you release the offenses and forgive each one. If you have trouble forgiving someone, try praying specifically for that person. Destroy the paper. Repeat this exercise as often as necessary.

_____
_____
_____
_____
_____
_____

Do you find it difficult to understand that you are God's treasure?

_____
_____
_____

Do you struggle with having compassion for others?

_____
_____
_____

Do you have trouble putting others first?

_____
_____
_____

How is your assignment different from your identity?

_____
_____
_____

CHAPTER NINETEEN

TOOLS... AND OPPORTUNITIES FOR MINISTRY

Congratulations, Coach! If you have completed this workbook, you have demonstrated you have the heart of a shepherd coach. Included in this chapter are resources and tools for you to use as you invest in the lives of your athletes.

RESOURCES

There are many resources available for Christian growth and discipleship, both in print and online. In recent years, various organizations have contributed material specifically written for athletes. Some are directed toward a specific sport and others target all athletes in general. It is helpful to have resources written in the language of the athlete.

Don't be afraid of technology, Coach! If you aren't familiar with online resources, it's likely several of your athletes are able to help. Don't hesitate to use their abilities!

It has been my privilege to be part of UPI, a ministry with professional baseball, for the past thirty-five years. Each staff member is a former pro athlete. The UPI GROW app is available on your phone or device and it is free. It has reached over ten thousand users so far. The app gives you several options:

- A daily challenge from the Word of God
- A weekly challenge from the Word of God
- Podcasts based on Bible studies with pro baseball teams
- Pitching instructional videos by MLB players Ian Kennedy, Luke Hocheaver, and Clayton Kershaw, including testimonies and a devotional taught by former MLB player Tony Graffanino

One of the best organizations in the baseball world is Baseball Chapel. Visit **www.baseballchapel.org** for resources for baseball players.

The following is a list of other organizations that work with athletes and provide good resources for discipleship:

- FCA
- AIA
- CHAPLAIN'S ROUND TABLE by OUR DAILY BREAD
- I AM SECOND
- INTERNATIONAL SPORTS COALITION
- THE INCREASE

Numerous athletes' testimonies are available on video apps like YouTube, which can be used during team Bible studies. There are several MLB players' stories of faith in video form on www.odb.org.

For coaches who desire to mentor and disciple their players, the following are additional suggested resources:

Possibly the best way to stay in touch with teams or individual athletes is either by text or email. If your setting allows, why not send a group text or email each day with an encouraging note or a Bible verse?

Email is a great tool for sharing your own teaching material, if you prefer. Some suggested topics are:

- Conflict Resolution
- Forgiveness
- How to Give a Testimony
- How to Share the Gospel
- How to Study the Bible

OTHER SUGGESTED TOOLS:

Skype
Marco Polo
Freeconferencecall.com
Facetime

SPORTS CARDS

Another idea to consider is printing a personal sports trading card! Many professional athletes have cards made with their picture in uniform on the front and a short testimony of their faith on the back. They often include a favorite Bible verse. Each time they are asked for an autograph, they can sign their card and it becomes an opportunity to share their faith.

Why not have your own cards made, Coach? They are inexpensive and a local printing company should be able make them. You could include your contact information on the back and use them as a tool for letting your community know about your faith, including your athletes, their parents, other students, recruits, fans and others. You may be uncomfortable with the idea, but it has been used effectively by many athletes as a ministry tool and it replaces a business card.

A sports card may also be a popular item with your athletes. They could trade them with each other and hand them out at team events and fundraisers. You, Coach, can disciple your athletes by setting the example in using this tool.

TAKING MINISTRY ON THE ROAD

Giving athletes opportunities to reach out to others can take their faith to the next level. As a young coach in northern Indiana, I took teams to Florida, Texas, Puerto Rico, Hawaii, and Russia. Why? I wanted to teach the athletes more than baseball. I wanted to give them a cross cultural experience where they could meet missionaries and interact with local people. With each trip, we would schedule work days and clinics, with opportunities to serve, share baseball, and speak about Jesus.

Trips are a great way to bond as a team. They not only increase our worldview but also allow us to put into action some of the things we have been learning. Even in a Christian college environment, I found very few athletes can articulate their faith or know how to share the gospel. A trip is a wonderful growth opportunity for your athletes to learn while doing. Think big, Coach! Think beyond your sport.

Obviously travel isn't always possible, especially in a public high school setting. However, there are still numerous ways for athletes to take ministry on the road. Check out opportunities in your community. Are there hospitals, orphanages, homeless shelters, soup kitchens, or retirement communities nearby?

There are many ways to serve others and be the hands and feet of Jesus. Most professional athletes have requirements in their contracts to participate in community events. Why not follow that model voluntarily?

KINDNESS

Another type of ministry is simple kindness. How about offering kindness to opponents? In baseball, the schedule often includes double headers. Spring weather in the Midwest is not always predictable. When opposing teams travel, why not make sure they have a comfortable place to go before and between games? How about providing food for them? I remember encouraging players to share their packed lunches, and not just the food they didn't like!

PROJECTS

Are there individuals in your community who are elderly, widowed, handicapped, or needy? What if your team donated a few hours to mow lawns or do other home maintenance? On one occasion, a team learned of a young woman who was hurting emotionally and financially. They noticed her house needed to be painted, so in two hours, the team scraped the entire house for her, preparing it for paint, and helping her reduce the cost. A few hours can make a huge difference!

YOUR TURN!

Are you overwhelmed by now? Guess what? You don't have to do all of it! These are just a few ideas to get you started. You have been given the unique opportunity to build up young men and women who will be warriors for the kingdom of God! The athletes you influence today can become influencers tomorrow. My prayer is that you will feel more equipped and excited to be leaders who disciple future leaders. That is the definition of a SHEPHERD COACH.

Which of these ideas can you implement to improve as a Shepherd Coach?

CHAPTER TWENTY
CHARTS

CHART A

PERSONAL MISSION STATEMENT

Go through each list quickly and circle three words from each column that best describe you.

LIST ONE

accomplish

acquire

adopt

advance

affect

affirm

alleviate

amplify

appreciate

ascend

associate

believe

bestow

brighten
build
call
cause
choose
claim
collect
combine
command
communicate
compel
compete
complete
compliment
compose
conceive
confirm
connect
consider
construct
contact
continue
counsel
create
decide
defend
delight

deliver
demonstrate
devise
direct
discuss
distribute
draft
dream
drive
educate
elect
embrace
encourage
endow
engage
enhance
enlighten
enlist
enliven
entertain
enthuse
evaluate
excite
explore
express
extend
facilitate

finance

forgive

foster

franchise

further

gather

generate

give

grant

heal

hold

host

LIST TWO

identify

illuminate

implement

improve

improvise

inspire

integrate

involve

keep

know

labor

launch

lead

light
live
love
make
manifest
master
measure
mediate
model
mold
motivate
move
negotiate
nurture
open
organize
participate
pass
perform
persuade
play
possess
practice
praise
prepare
present
produce

progress
promise
promote
provide
pursue

LIST THREE

realize
receive
reclaim
reduce
refine
reflect
reform
regards
relate
relax
release
rely
remember
renew
resonate
restore
return
revise
sacrifice
safeguard

satisfy

save

sell

serve

share

speak

stand

summon

support

surrender

sustain

take care

tap

team

touch

trade

translate

travel

understand

use

utilize

validate

value

venture

verbalize

volunteer

work

write

yield

Write down the three most meaningful, purposeful, and exciting verbs from your circled words:

_____, _____, and _____.

These three verbs comprise Puzzle Piece #1.

What do you stand for? What principle, cause, value, or purpose would you be willing to defend to the death or devote your life to? For example, some people's key phrase or value might reflect joy, service, justice, family, creativity, freedom, equality, faith, or excellence.

What is your core? Write the word phrase down here:

_____

This is Puzzle Piece #2.

Whom are you here to empower, assist, and impact? Write it here:

_____

This is Puzzle Piece #3.

SHEPHERD COACH

THIS IS THE FORMULA FOR YOUR PERSONAL MISSION STATEMENT!

(Puzzle Piece #1 + Puzzle Piece #2 to, for, or with Puzzle #3)

My mission is to:
_____, _____, and _____
(your three verbs)
(Puzzle Piece #1)

_____ (your core value or values)
(Puzzle Piece #2)

to, for, or with
_____ (the group/cause which most moves/excites you)
(Puzzle Piece #3)

CHART B

OVERVIEW OF WHO YOU ARE

What sports are you currently coaching?
_____
_____
_____

What sports do you feel qualified to coach?
_____
_____

What sports did you play competitively? (circle)
- Grade school
- High school
- College
- Pro
- Intramural

Who is the favorite coach you played for and why was he a favorite?
_____
_____
_____

Who was your least favorite coach and why?
_____
_____
_____

What qualities would you like to copy from these coaches?
_____
_____
_____

Do you feel you have been biblically discipled? Please explain how and anything you feel appropriate to your personal study of your spiritual journey.

_____
_____
_____

What spiritual activities do you currently do with or for your team?

_____
_____
_____

RECCOMENDED VIDEO RESOURCE:

2:20 SECOND YOUTUBE VIDEO ENTITLED **WHY WE COACH** ON YOUTUBE: **YOUTUBE.COM/WATCH?V=CGNAM6_DYMU**

MEET THE AUTHOR

Tom Roy was the president and is founder of Unlimited Potential Inc., a ministry to professional baseball players. He has been a voice in major league baseball for almost 4 decades. Tom also served as a head high school baseball coach for three years as well as having 15 years coaching experience as a pitching coach and head coach at the college level. Tom and his wife, Carin, Live in Winona Lake, Indiana and are the parents of two adult daughters.

MORE FROM TOM ROY:

RELEASED
A story of God's Power Released in Pro Baseball

BEYOND BETRAYAL
(co-authored with Jerry Price)

SANDUSKY BAY
(co-authored with Jerry Price)

ELLISON BAY
(co-authored with Jerry Price)

LAKE OF BAYS
(co-authored with Jerry Price)

TO CONNECT WITH TOM ROY
VISIT ONLINE OR **WRITE TO**:

1247 FREEDOM PARKWAY

WINONA LAKE, INDIANA 46590

TOMROY.NET

FOR VOLUME DISCOUNTS OF THIS BOOK FOR YOU OR YOUR ORGANIZATION CONTACT:

PULPIT TO PAGE PUBLISHING CO.

ORDERS@PULPITTOPAGE.COM

PULPITTOPAGE.COM

Made in the USA
Columbia, SC
17 April 2019